# SKY SPIRIT

## A Collection of Works, Poems and Quotes

By

## TWO FEATHERS

*Ronald David Shaw*

# *SKY SPIRIT*

## A Collection of Works, Poems and Quotes

© 2018 by Ronald David Shaw
Eastern Band Cherokee

First Publication:

Published in the United States of America

Published by
ATC Publishing LLC
P.O. Box 127
Senoia, Georgia 30276

ISBN-13: 978-0-9990607-4-2
ISBN-10: 0-9990607-4-0

# TABLE OF CONTENTS

## INTRODUCTION

# Introduction

Ronald David Shaw, Eastern Band Cherokee

His Lineage began with the marriage of his Great Grandfather William B. Smith to Miley Brown, Eastern Band Cherokee.

William was a Doctor who lived with the Cherokee, worked with them, and learned many of their ways and as a doctor studied healing herbs from the Medicine Men. His Daughter, Sabra Amanda Jane Smith also followed her father's work as his assistant, later worked as a Medicine Woman among the Cherokee and learned enough to create a book of cures and remedies passed down to his family.

Ron has studied their history along with the Cherokee People, their stories, traditions and Spiritual Ways which he keeps alive in his work and in his person.

*In the breeze of the morning sun, Lift your hands up to the sky,*
*Let your heart feel the Love of our Great Father up Above.*

*Ronald David Shaw*

# PART 1

# SKY SPIRIT

### GREAT SPIRIT

*I LOOK ACROSS THE VALLEY DEEP AND WIDE, THE TALL*
*MOUNTAINS STANDING SIDE BY SIDE.*
*THE WIND BLOWS THRU MY HAIR, I CAN FEEL THE SPIRIT OF*
*BROTHER BEAR.*
*I USE THE SPIRITS TO GUIDE ME THRU LIKE THE MAGIC*
*WATERS CRYSTAL BLUE.*
*SOMETIMES I WONDER HOW FAR I CAN GO. THE GREAT*
*SPIRIT SAYS TAKE IT SLOW.*
*AS I TRAVEL THESE TRAILS TILL THE END, I HOPE I'VE MADE*
*A FRIEND THRU LIFE'S BEND.*
*I END THESE WORDS FROM MY HEART, I KNOW THE GREAT*
*SPIRIT WILL NEVER DEPART.*

# *WONDERING BRAVE*

*As the eagle flies across the sky, I often wonder what*

*he sees with his eyes.*

*Is it the mountain covered with snow, or is it the*

*winding river flowing pure and slow?*

*Does the great Eagle see brother bear, standing with*

*strength and courage as wind blows thru his hair?*

*And does the Eagle hear the Buffalo going across the*

*Plains like the sound of thunder or heavy rains*

*and see the many stars that shine at night just like*

*our people once was, proud and full of life.*

*As I travel these trails, I will learn all things so my*

*life will be full of wisdom, strength and kindness.*

*As I sit by the river alone, I can hear the whisper of*

*the Elk and the Deer and it tells me not to fear.*

*For life is short and sometimes not clear.*

*I take all things that I have learned and put them in*

*my heart not to be burned but to be set free for all to*

*see.*

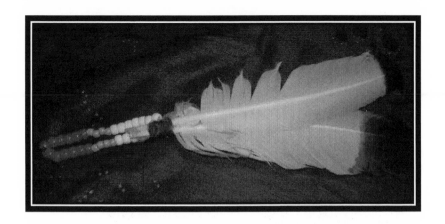

*TWO FEATHERS*

*TWO FEATHERS I WEAR WITH PRIDE.*

*TWO FEATHERS TIED SIDE BY SIDE.*

*TWO FEATHERS THAT BLOW IN THE WIND, MY DEEP PRAYERS*

*TO THE GREAT SPIRIT I SEND.*

*TWO FEATHERS IS MY INDIAN NAME, SHOW ME RESPECT AND*

*I WILL SHOW YOU THE SAME.*

LOVE,

        CHERISH,

                HONOR

*ALL THINGS BOTH GREAT AND SMALL.*

## VISION

*THE GRASS SEEMS VERY GREEN ON THE OTHER SIDE*

*BY THE RIVER DEEP AND WIDE.*

*THE INDIAN PONIES GRAZE IN THE VALLEY BELOW*

*AS I LOOK AT THE MOUNTAIN TOPS FULL OF SNOW.*

*I DRIFT OFF TO A DREAM I ONCE HAD*

*IT WAS GOOD AND NEVER BAD.*

*I WAS DREAMING OF A PLACE WHERE WILD HORSES RUN FREE.*

*IT'S SO BEAUTIFUL JUST TO SEE.*

*I ALSO SEE THE GREAT CHIEFS WITH THEIR FEATHERS*

*BLOWING IN THE WIND.*

**PROUD SPIRITS,**

**MY BROTHERS,**

**MY FRIENDS.**

# SPIRIT OF THE WIND

*YOU ARE IN THE SPIRIT OF THE WIND. I HEAR YOUR VOICE.*

*YOU ARE IN THE SPIRIT OF THE SUN. I FEEL THE WARMTH OF YOUR LOVE.*

*YOU ARE IN THE SPIRIT OF THE FIRE THAT BURNS DEEP INTO MY SOUL.*

*YOU ARE IN THE SPIRIT OF THE WATER. FROM YOU I DRINK AND QUENCH MY THIRST.*

*I HAVE ALWAYS LOVED YOU.*

## THE ANGEL

*AS AN ANGEL APPEARED ON A MIDNIGHT CLEAR*
*I STOOD ALONE SHEDDING A TEAR.*
*SHE STOOD THERE AND STARED AT ME, HER EYES A PEACEFUL*
*GLOW*
*I DID NOT HAVE TO SPEAK BECAUSE SHE KNOWS WHAT I*
*KNOW.*
*SHE COULD FEEL WHAT I'D KEPT DEEP INSIDE AND*
*SAID "DON'T LEAVE IT THERE TO HIDE.*
*SHE SAID "OPEN YOUR ARMS, FEEL THE WIND*
*LIKE A FREE BIRD ON A SUMMERS DAY.*
*LOOK DEEP INTO MY EYES FOR I WILL SHOW YOU THE WAY.*

*NEVER GIVE UP ON*
*YOUR HOPES AND*
*DREAMS*
*FOR THERE WILL*
*COME A DAY IT WILL*
*BE AS IT SEEMS."*

## HEAL MY BROTHER

*GREAT SPIRIT, I COME TO YOU WITH A PURE HEART. I ASK YOU TO BLESS MY FAMILY AND TO HELP US EACH DAY. I ALSO ASK THAT YOU TOUCH MY BROTHER AND HEAL HIM. GIVE HIM A LONG HAPPY LIFE. FOR I WILL ALWAYS LOVE MY BROTHER.*

# PART 2

## *FOR MY LADY*

### *WHEN I LOOK INTO YOUR EYES*

*WHEN I LOOK INTO YOUR EYES*
*OR FEEL YOUR BREATH UPON MY SKIN*
*FROM EACH TOUCH AND EACH KISS*
*THERE IS SO MUCH LOVE.*
*I SHALL ALWAYS LOVE, HONOR, CHERISH AND RESPECT YOU.*
*YOU ARE IN MY EVERY THOUGHT, MY HEART AND MY SOUL.*

### *SMILE*

THE SUN CANNOT OUT SHINE YOUR BEAUTIFUL SMILE.
I HOPE YOU DON'T MIND IF I SIT AWHILE.
YOUR FINGERS ARE LIKE MAGIC SENT FROM ABOVE
SOFT AND TENDER AS A SNOW-WHITE DOVE.
YOUR LIPS ARE LIKE CHERRIES DANCING IN THE WIND.
I WANT TO HOLD YOU CLOSE TILL THE VERY END.

## ON THE DOCK

*I SIT ON THE DOCK AND LOOK ACROSS THE LAKE EVEN BEFORE YOU ARE AWAKE.*

*THERE IS A GENTLE BREEZE BLOWING HERE. THE WIND WHISPERS YOUR LOVE IS ALWAYS NEAR.*

*I CLOSE MY EYES AND SEE YOUR FACE SO BEAUTIFUL HERE IN THIS PLACE.*

*I CALL OUT YOUR NAME AND GIVE IT TO MY SPIRIT. HE WILL CARRY IT TO YOUR HEART AND YOU WILL ALSO HEAR IT.*

*THE LOVE I HAVE IS DEEP AND TRUE AND ONLY MEANT FOR YOU.*

*TWO FEATHERS, BLOWING IN THE WIND, MAY NEVER SEE LOVE TO THE END.*

*HOLD ON TIGHT, HOLD ON TRUE, ALL THIS LOVE IS FOR YOU.*

*OPEN YOUR EYES FOR THIS IS A NEW DAY. LISTEN WHAT MY HEART HAS TO SAY.*

*YOU WALKED INTO MY HEART THROUGH AN OPEN DOOR. NOW I LOVE YOU MORE AND MORE.*

*YOU GAVE ME YOUR HAND AND PROMISED TO BE TRUE, THE ONLY ONE I LOVE IS YOU.*

*TAKE MY HEART. TAKE MY SOUL. MY LOVE WILL BE THERE WHEN WE GROW OLD.*

# IN THIS DREAM

*IF YOU GO TO SLEEP AND HAVE A DREAM,*

*AND YOU SEE ME BY A MOUNTAIN STREAM.*

*IF YOU REALLY LOOK DEEP INSIDE*

*I DON'T HAVE ANYTHING TO HIDE.*

*I HAVE A PEACEFUL AND TENDER HEART*

*AND IT SOMETIMES BREAKS WHEN WE'RE APART.*

*SO IF YOU DON'T THINK I WAS THE BEST*

*JUST LEAVE ME HERE IN THIS DREAM.*

*YOU CAN HAVE THE REST*

*IF YOU GO TO SLEEP AND HAVE MY DREAM,*

*YOU SEE ME BY A MOUNTAIN STREAM.*

*YOU LOOK ACROSS AND INTO MY EYES,*

*YOU SEE LOVE AND NO LIES.*

*SO, REACH OUT YOUR HAND AND PLACE IT IN MINE,*

*I WILL LOVE YOU THROUGHOUT TIME.*

*I'VE BEEN JUDGED LIKE A BOOK BUT PLEASE*

*TAKE A SECOND LOOK.*

*IF YOU WANT TO HAVE THIS DREAM TO COME TRUE,*

*KISS ME, HOLD ME. I LOVE YOU.*

## My Feelings

*I WISH I COULD TOUCH YOUR FACE,*

*IT LOOKS SOFT AND BEAUTIFUL AS FINE LACE.*

*I WISH I COULD FEEL WHAT'S IN YOUR HEART*

*WHEN WE ARE CLOSE AND WHEN WE ARE APART.*

*I WISH I COULD HOLD YOUR HAND AS WE*

*WALK ALONG THE BEACH IN THE SAND.*

*I WISH I COULD BE THERE WHEN YOU SHED A TEAR.*

*I WOULD HOLD YOU CLOSE SO YOU WOULD HAVE NO FEAR.*

*I WISH I COULD TAKE AWAY ALL OF THE PAIN,*

*PUT IT IN A BOTTLE AND THROW IT INTO THE HARDEST RAIN.*

*I WISH I COULD KISS YOUR LIPS OF SWEET WINE,*

*THEN ONE DAY YOU WILL SAY YOU WOULD BE MINE.*

# MY YELLOW ROSE

*DOES ANYBODY KNOW MY YELLOW ROSE?*

*DOES ANYBODY KNOW MY YELLOW ROSE, THE ONE THAT REACHES OUT AND TOUCHES MY VERY SOUL.*
*DOES ANYBODY KNOW MY YELLOW ROSE? SHE IS THE ONE WHO MADE LIFE WORTH LIVING.*
*DOES ANYBODY KNOW MY YELLOW ROSE? THE ONE WHO MAKES ME HUNGER FOR HER LOVE.*
*DOES ANYBODY KNOW MY YELLOW ROSE? THE ONE WHO LOVED ME FOR WHO I AM.*
*DOES ANYBODY KNOW MY YELLOW ROSE? SHE IS THE ONE I BELIEVE IN.*
*I WILL STAND BESIDE HER TO THE VERY END.*
*YOU WOULD ONLY WISH TO KNOW MY YELLOW ROSE. SHE IS ONE OF A KIND, ONE IN A MILLION, ONE IN MY LIFE AND*

*I DO LOVE MY YELLOW ROSE.*

# *YOU ARE MY DREAM*

*YOU ARE MY DREAM AND I AM THE DREAMER.*

*YOU ARE THE STARS AND I AM THE MIDNIGHT SKY.*

*YOU ARE THE RISING SUN AND YOU ARE THE ONLY ONE.*

*YOU ARE THE ONE I WILL REACH FOR*

*YOU ARE THE ONLY ONE I WILL ADORE.*

*YOU ARE THE ONE THAT MAKES ME SMILE*

*I WILL GO THE EXTRA MILE.*

*YOU ARE THE ONE OF MY LIFE*

*ONE DAY YOU WILL BE MY WIFE.*

# *MY WIFE*

*I WILL HONOR YOU ALL THE DAYS OF OUR LIVES.*

*WE- HONOR EARTH, FOR OUR MARRIAGE TO BE ABUNDANT*

*AS WE WALK THROUGH LIFE.*

*WE- HONOR FIRE FOR OUR UNION TO BE WARM AND*

*GLOWING WITH LOVE.*

*WE- HONOR WIND THAT WE MAY SAIL THROUGH LIFE, SAFE*

*AND CALM AS IN THE GREAT SPIRITS ARMS.*

*WE- HONOR WATER TO CLEAN AND SMOOTH OUR MARRIAGE,*

*THAT IT MAY NEVER THIRST FOR LOVE.*

# PART 3

# *DEEP THOUGHTS*

## *THE WAY I AM*

*THE WAY I AM IS: KINDNESS. KINDNESS COMES FROM MY HEART. THE WORD'S I SPEAK COME OUT WITH MEANING AND UNDERSTANDING.*

*THE WAY I AM IS: CARING. CARING ALSO COMES FROM MY HEART SO I CAN UNDERSTAND WHAT A PERSON IS GOING THROUGH, TO LISTEN TO WHAT THEY HAVE TO SAY AND HELP IF I CAN.*

*THE WAY I AM IS: STRENGTH. TO HOLD SOMEONE, TO HAVE A SHOULDER TO LEAN ON, TO CRY ON, TO BE THERE IF NEEDED.*

*THE WAY I AM IS: TENDERNESS. WITH A HUG, A SMILE OR A SOFT-SPOKEN WORD JUST TO MAKE SOMEONE SMILE OR LAUGH.*

*ALL THESE THINGS I WANT TO BE AND*
*ALL THESE WORDS I SHALL KEEP.*

## *The Well – Remembering When*

*We grew up on an old dirt road in Coweta county Georgia.*

*We had no running water to the house however we had a well from which we drew water with a bucket.*

*I remember my Mother always said, you have to give in order to get.*

*Well, I thought about that... so you have to give an effort in drawing that bucket of water up from that 30 foot well.*

*Later on I thought about it some more... you learn you get more from that bucket than just water.*

*If someone walked up, you would offer them a drink.*

*So, you learn to share. And... by giving them the first drink you also learn respect and compassion.*

*I also learned it is not just the water, you can draw from many things ...*

*Like... what you see or where you have been. Draw from it and look for the good.*

*Yes, that old bucket of water can teach you many lessons.*

*DON'T MAKE QUICK DECISIONS. JUST THINK OF WHAT GOOD THAT DAY HAS BROUGHT. BY LOWERING THE BUCKET DOWN IN THE WELL, YOU LET IF FILL ... JUST LIKE OPENING YOUR HEART TO SOMEONE IN NEED AND LET IF FILL. EACH TIME YOU LEARN THERE IS MUCH MORE IN THAT BUCKET THAN JUST WATER.*

*I WAS BLESSED WITH MY WIFE FOR FOURTEEN YEARS AND WITH HER MY BUCKET WAS ALWAYS FULL WITH LOVE, UNDERSTANDING, COMPASSION, RESPECT AND HONOR. I DRAW FROM MY BUCKET EVERY DAY TO KEEP IT FULL. EVERYONE HAS A BUCKET SO TRY TO THINK OF THINGS TO KEEP IT FULL AND GOD WILL BLESS!*

## *YOU ARE THE ANGEL*

*YOU ARE THE ANGEL THAT LIFTS MY SPIRIT.*
*YOU ARE THE ANGEL THAT TOUCHES MY SOUL.*
*YOU ARE THE ANGEL THAT BREATHES UPON MY SKIN AND GIVES ME NEW LIFE.*

## TEAR DROP

SOMETIMES IN LIFE NO MATTER AS A BABY OR AN ADULT WE
ALL HAVE TEARS.
SOME MAY BE HAPPY SOME MAY BE SAD, BUT EACH TEAR
DROP CAN MEAN MANY DIFFERENT THINGS.
SOME SCARED, SOME MAD AND SOME HURT.
IN MY LIFE I'VE HAD MANY, BUT EACH TEAR HAD A PURPOSE.
IF I EVER MADE YOU CRY I WANT TO BE THERE TO CATCH THE
LAST TEAR DROP AND PUT IT IN MY HEART
SO I WILL UNDERSTAND AND NOT MAKE YOU CRY AGAIN.
FOR WITH YOUR PAIN IS MY PAIN.


## HEAR THE SILENCE

CAN YOU HEAR THE SILENCE OF THE NIGHT
UNDER THE PALE MOON LIGHT?
I LOOK OUT MY WINDOW AND SEE THE RAIN,
BUT IN MY HEART I STILL FEEL THE PAIN.
IT GOES ON BOTH DAY AND NIGHT,
SOMETIMES I WANT TO GIVE UP THE FIGHT
SOMETHING TELLS ME, 'PRESS ON
YOU WON'T HAVE TO WAIT LONG.'

# ME

*WHAT IS IT WITH ME OR*

*WHAT DO THE PEOPLE REALLY SEE.*

*IS IT THE TATTOOS UPON MY ARM?*

*THEY ARE OK AND I MEAN NO HARM.*

*I AM NOT JUST AN AVERAGE GUY.*

*I HAVE A HEART AND SOMETIMES I CRY.*

*IT'S NOT THAT I AM WEAK AND CONFUSED*

*I'M JUST TIRED OF BEING PLAYED AND USED.*

*I OPEN MY HEART FOR THOSE IN NEED*

*WITH MY KINDNESS I HOPE TO PLANT A SEED.*


## I BUILD A WALL

*I BUILD A WALL BOTH BIG AND TALL*
*TO PROTECT MY HEART FROM THEM ALL.*

## FRIENDS

*A FRIEND LIKE YOU IS VERY SPECIAL TO ME.*
*AS BY THE SMILE ON MY FACE YOU CAN SEE.*
*FRIENDS ARE NOT TO GIVE EACH OTHER HURT AND PAIN*
*BUT TO LIFT EACH OTHER UP DESPITE THE RAIN.*
*SOMETIMES IT FEELS LIKE IT'S HARD TO WIN A RACE*
*AND YOU FEEL LIKE YOU'RE IN 2ND PLACE.*
*A FRIEND COMES ALONG TO LEND A HAND*
*THEN YOU ARE NUMBER ONE AND THAT'S VERY GRAND.*

## MAN WITH A HEART

*THERE ONCE WAS A MAN WITH A HEART OF GOLD.*
*EVERYONE TREATED HIM VERY COLD.*
*HE ALWAYS KEPT A SMILE ON HIS FACE*
*BECAUSE HE KNEW IT WAS NO DISGRACE.*
*HE LOVED AND CARED FOR THE PEOPLE HE MET.*
*IN HIS WAYS HE WAS SET.*
*NO CHANGES IN HIM COULD THE PEOPLE SEE.*
*"DON'T BE AFRAID, IT'S ONLY ME."*
*I OPEN MY ARMS TO FEEL THE LOVE, IF NOT FROM HERE,*
*SURELY FROM ABOVE.*

# I WISH

I WISH I COULD FEEL WHAT YOU FEEL INSIDE. DO I NEED TO
STAND OR GO SOMEWHERE AND HIDE?
I WISH I COULD SEE WHAT YOUR EYES REALLY SEE. I AM
DIFFERENT BUT IT'S ONLY ME.
I WISH I COULD TOUCH YOUR HEART LIKE YOU'VE TOUCHED
MINE. YOU WOULD SEE IT'S NOT A CRIME.
I TRY SO HARD AT THINGS I DO,
WHAT I WISH FOR MAY ONE DAY COME TRUE.

# ALL I NEED

ALL I NEED IS A FRIEND LIKE YOU,
AND IF YOU NEED ME I WILL BE THERE FOR YOU.
ALL I NEED IS TO TAKE ONE DAY AT A TIME,
AND KEEP EVERYTHING CLEAR ON MY MIND.
ALL I NEED IS ONE STAR, ONE HOPE AND ONE DREAM
TO PLACE THEM ALL BY A QUIET STREAM.
THEN I CAN VISIT THEM FROM TIME TO TIME,
TO REMEMBER WHAT WAS ON MY MIND.
ALL I NEED IS A FRIEND LIKE YOU, BECAUSE YOU'RE THE BEST
NOT LIKE THE REST.

## WHY

*WHY DO I DO THE THINGS I DO, OR*
*WHY DO I FEEL SO BLUE?*
*HAVE I SAID OR DONE SOMETHING TO HURT SOMEONE?*
*IF I DID IT WAS A MISTAKE AND NOT FOR FUN.*


## STAR WISH

*I LOOK OUT ACROSS THE MIDNIGHT SKY, I PICK OUT A STAR*
*THAT PUTS A TWINKLE IN MY EYE.*
*I WISH UPON IT SOFT AND LOW THEN IT LIGHTS UP WITH A*
*GLOW.*
*WHAT I WISH FOR, BOTH BIG AND SMALL, IT COMES FROM MY*
*HEART. THAT'S ALL.*
*SOMETIMES MY WISHES THEY DO COME TRUE, ALL I NEED IS*
*ONE, THE REST I GIVE TO YOU.*
*USE THEM WISELY WITH LOVE AND AFFECTION,*
*THEN IT WILL SHOW YOU THE RIGHT DIRECTION.*

# NIGHTFALL

*As nightfall comes with each passing day*

*I look up to the heavens and this I say.*

*I wish upon a star so bright*

*I hope my wish comes true tonight.*

*All I ask for in this old life*

*is to be humble and caring without any strife.*

*In this world there's lots of heartache, trouble and*

*pain,*

*but as long as I can smile and say a kind word*

*maybe I can help chase away the rain.*

*Sometimes I look at my own life and feel sad.*

*Does anyone care for me or am I too bad.*

*If I'm sitting and shed a tear it's not because of some*

*fear*

*it's because I've done my best for another year.*

## *THINKING BEYOND*

*TO DREAM THE IMPOSSIBLE DREAM TO HAVE THAT DREAM*

*COME TRUE.*

*TO HAVE AN UNCONDITIONAL LOVE AND TO HAVE IT WITHOUT*

*CONDITIONS.*

*TO SEE WHAT WE REALLY FEEL AND TO FEEL WHAT WE SEE IN*

*EACH OTHER.*

*TO TOUCH SOMEONE THAT YOU BELIEVE IN*

*AND TO BELIEVE IN THE ONE YOU TOUCH.*

*TO KISS YOU IN A MOMENT*

*IS A MOMENT OF WONDERFUL MEMORIES.*

*TO SPEAK OF WHAT YOU WANT IN LIFE*

*IS TO HAVE THE VERY THING THAT LOVE BRINGS.*

*FROM THIS DAY FORWARD,*

*SPEAK LOVE. DREAM THAT DREAM*

*REACH OUT AND TOUCH IT. BELIEVE IN IT. HOLD ON TO IT.*

*NEVER LET IT GO. KISS THE KISS OF THAT VERY FIRST KISS.*

## *I Believe -*

*I believe -*

> *In the things that are important to you*
> *and how you accomplish anything you set out to do.*

### *I believe -*

> *That you have what it takes. To overcome obstacles*
> *and grow from every experience life brings your way.*

### *I believe -*

> *In your courage, compassion and strength of*
> *character.*

### *I believe -*

> *In your Goodness and our close friendship.*

### *I believe in you!*

# *THE MOON WAS FULL*

*THE MOON WAS FULL ON THIS COOL FALL NIGHT.*

*THE WOLVES HOWLED TILL THE MORNING LIGHT.*

*I PICKED UP SOME STICKS AND STONES THEN MIXED THEM*

*WITH SOME OLD BONES.*

*I LOOKED UP TO THE HEAVENS AND SAID A PRAYER*

*I DID NOT SWEAR.*

*IF I MAY OR IF I MIGHT, SHOW ME THE GUIDING LIGHT.*

*THE LIGHT CAME AND WENT ACROSS THE SKY.*

*IT PUT A GLEAM IN MY EYE.*

*I SEARCHED SHORT AND I SEARCHED LONG*

*HOPING TO FIND WHERE I BELONG.*

*WHEN OUR EYES MET, IT WAS SET IN STONE*

*WE WILL HAVE A HAPPY HOME.*

## To Dream the Impossible

### Thinking Beyond

To dream the impossible dream, To have that dream
come true.

To have an unconditional love, and to love without
conditions.

To see what we really feel, and to feel what we see
in each other.

To touch someone that you believe in, and to believe
in the one you touch.

To kiss you in a moment is a moment of wonderful
memories.

To speak of what you want in life is to have the very
thing that love brings.

From this day forward, you speak love, you dream
that dream, you reach out and touch it, believe in it,
hold to it, and never let go.

Kiss the kiss of that very first kiss.

All of this is yours.

# MEMORIES AND NOW

*SITTING IN THE SILENCE, BY THE WATER SO CALM.*

*I SURE DO MISS YOU AND I LOVE YOU MOM.*

*I ENJOYED SITTING AT THE TABLE AND TALKING ABOUT THE*

*TIMES WE HAD*

*SOME WAS GOOD AND SOME WAS SAD.*

*SOMETIMES I FEEL SO OUT OF PLACE*

*I TRY NOT TO SHOW IT ON MY FACE.*

*THIS HURT I HAVE REALLY GETS OLD*

*AND IT GOES DEEP INTO MY SOUL.*

*WHAT HAVE I EVER DONE TO FEEL SO ALONE.*

*SOMETIMES I WANT TO GIVE UP AND COME HOME.*

*I BELIEVE IN THE SPIRITS AND THEY TOUCH MY HEART.*

*THEY TELL ME HOLD ON FOR THERE IS ANOTHER PART.*

# Words of Truth

*The sky is blue, the clouds are white,*

*Just as pure as my heart is for you tonight.*

*The valleys are deep, and the mountains tall,*

*I give my everything and my love that's all.*

*You said you would always be true,*

*I believe that because it came from you.*

*Every time I look at you and see your beauty and*

*love,*

*It reminds me of a pure white dove sent from above.*

*I will love you my dear throughout the years.*

*With me you should have no more tears.*

*I will do things both big and small.*

*It comes from my heart and my all.*

*All the words we speak will make a stand.*

*Love sure is Grand.*

*From your first touch I knew I loved you so much.*

*Baby your kiss is so fine,*

*I'm very thankful you're mine.*

## SILENCE

SOMETIMES SILENCE CAN BE SO LOUD MY HEART BEATS LIKE
THUNDER.
I CLOSE MY EYES AND TAKE A DEEP BREATH.
TO REMEMBER, NEVER DOUBT, BUT BELIEVE IN WHAT CAN BE.
MY FEELINGS SLIP OUT OF MY EYES.


## DREAMER

YOU ARE THE DREAM AND I AM THE DREAMER.
YOU ARE THE STARS AND I AM THE MIDNIGHT SKY.
I REACH OUT MY HAND JUST TO FEEL YOUR TOUCH
YOU DON'T KNOW HOW I WANT TO HOLD YOU SO MUCH.
I LOOK AT YOUR EYES AS YOU LOOK INTO MINE.
IT PUTS ME INTO A TRANCE AS I GO BACK INTO TIME.
I WISH THIS DREAM COULD BE REAL
THEN I WOULD KNOW HOW YOU REALLY FEEL.
SOMETIME I WISH UPON A FALLING STAR
THAT MY DREAM WOULD NOT BE SO FAR.

## NOT PROMISED TOMORROW

*IN LIFE WE ARE NOT PROMISED TOMORROW, BUT I HOPE TO TELL YOU IN MY LAST BREATH, I LOVE YOU.*

*THE THINGS THAT ARE TRUE, WAS MY LOVE FOR YOU, AND IT HAS ALWAYS BEEN. I WOULD LOVE TO HOLD YOU AND KISS YOU ONE LAST TIME.*

*I HAVE ALWAYS DONE MY BEST TO SHOW YOU LOVE AND HAPPINESS, FOR EVERY BEAT OF MY HEART WAS FOR YOU.*

*YOU HAVE ALWAYS BEEN THERE WITH ME AND WALKED THROUGH LIFE WITH ME. I WILL REMEMBER YOUR BEAUTIFUL SMILE.*

*LOOK AT ME AND REMEMBER ME AS I ALWAYS WAS.*

*MY WORDS AND MY LOVE WILL ALWAYS BE WITH YOU.*

*AT THE END OF MY DAY, REMEMBER THE GOOD TIMES AND OUR MEMORIES.*

*KEEP MY LETTERS OF LOVE TO YOU AND MY LOVE THAT IS EACH ONE.*

*FOR MY LOVE WILL ALWAYS BE WITH YOU.*

## LAST WORDS

*WHEN I TRAVEL THESE TRAILS OF DEATH,*

*I HOPE TO HAVE ONE LAST BREATH.*

*TO TELL YOU THINGS THAT ARE TRUE.*

*TO HUG YOU, HOLD YOU AND BE WITH YOU.*

*I HAVE ALWAYS TRIED TO BE PRECIOUS AND SWEET,*

*SO YOU COULD FEEL IT IN MY EVERY HEARTBEAT.*

*YOU HAVE BEEN THERE WITH ME AND WALKED THE MILE.*

*I WILL ALWAYS REMEMBER YOUR BEAUTIFUL SMILE.*

*SO AS THE SUN SETS ON MY LAST DAY*

*PLEASE CAST YOUR EYES MY WAY.*

*KEEP MY WORDS AND MY HEART*

*FOR MY LOVE WILL NEVER DEPART.*

*"WITH YOUR LOVE, I LIVE ANOTHER DAY"*

## SPIRIT WORLD

*HAVE YOU EVER WONDERED ABOUT THE SPIRIT WORLD OR WHERE IT IS?*

*IT COULD BE RIGHT HERE. NO ONE KNOWS FOR SURE.*

*LET ME TELL YOU... IT IS REAL, JUST LIKE YOU AND I.*

*EVER ON A SUMMER DAY HAVE YOU FELT A COLD CHILL OR SEEN A SHADOW, LOOKED BACK AND IT WAS GONE. YOU THINK IT WAS JUST YOUR IMAGINATION... OR WAS IT?*

*HAVE YOU EVER CLOSED YOUR EYES AND THOUGHT BACK IN TIME OF A LOVED ONE, THEN HEAR THEIR LAUGHTER OR HEAR THEIR WORDS WHEN THEY TELL YOU THEY LOVE YOU.*

*MEMORIES OF THE PAST ARE STILL HERE AROUND YOU ...*

*TODAY.*

# DISTANT DRUMS

*I HEAR THE DRUM BEAT FROM A DISTANT MOUNTAIN.*

*IT ECHOES IN ALL DIRECTIONS.*

*AS THE DRUM BEATS, IT SENDS A MESSAGE FOR ALL TO LISTEN.*

*THEY SPEAK OF REFLECTIONS AND COURAGE OF ONE'S SELF TO DO THE RIGHT THING IN ORDER TO MOVE THROUGH LIFE.*

*AS THE DRUM STILL BEATS, IT SPEAKS OF AN ETERNAL LIFE, AS SPIRIT WORLD WHERE ALL THINGS AREA FREE OF SICKNESS, PAIN AND EVEN DEATH.*

*WE ALL HAVE A DRUM INSIDE OF US AND WE MUST FOLLOW OUR HEART, FOR ALL THINGS WILL COME FULL CIRCLE.*

*MAY GOD BLESS ALL THAT LISTEN TO THAT DRUM.*

## PRAYER TO SKY SPIRIT

GREAT SPIRIT...

I COME TO YOU WITH OPEN HEART AND OPEN ARMS.

THE LAST WEEK I HAVE HAD A LOT ON MY MIND AND ON MY HEART.

I ASK YOU GREAT SPIRIT TO SHOW ME THE PATH I NEED TO TAKE.

GREAT SPIRIT GIVE ME STRENGTH AND COURAGE TO MAKE EACH STEP.

I WANT TO LEARN FROM YOU EACH DAY PATIENCE AND WISDOM.

I ALWAYS NEED YOU IN MY HEART SO I MAY SHOW REFLECTIONS OF WHAT YOU TEACH.

SHOW ME OPTIONS OF THE WAY I MAY GO AND THE PATH THAT I MAY FOLLOW.

SHOW ME THE BRIGHT SUNSET AND KEEP EACH IN MY HEART.

AND EVEN THE SHADOWS OF MY REFLECTION WILL NOT BE FORGOTTEN.

THANK YOU, ALWAYS... GREAT SPIRIT.

### *Dreaming of You*

*I was just dreaming of you as we held hands next to a*

*quiet running stream.*

*I was Dreaming of you, as you said*

*I am falling in love*

*I was dreaming of you*

*as we had our first kiss.*

*I was Dreaming of you as we walked through a*

*garden, where butterflies were as beautiful as you.*

*I was dreaming of you when you told me, I love you*

*I was dreaming of you when you said it was time to go.*

*I was dreaming of you when I told you I love you*

*And gave you our last kiss.*

*I was dreaming of you*

*'In Memory of Elizabeth Shaw'*
*03/20/1960 – 07/12/2019*

## GREAT SPIRIT

*AS I TRAVEL THESE TRAILS TILL THE END, I HOPE I'VE MADE*
*A FRIEND THRU LIFE'S BEND.*
*I END THESE WORDS FROM MY HEART AS I KNOW THE GREAT*
*SPIRIT WILL NEVER DEPART.* *RON SHAW*

# TEN COMMANDMENTS FROM THE GREAT SPIRIT

1. THE EARTH IS OUR MOTHER, CARE FOR HER

2. HONOR ALL RELATIONS

3. OPEN YOUR HEART AND SOUL TO THE GREAT SPIRIT

4. ALL LIFE IS SACRED. TREAT ALL BEINGS WITH RESPECT

5. TAKE FROM THE EARTH ONLY WHAT IS NEEDED. NOTHING ELSE.

6. DO WHAT NEEDS TO BE DONE FOR THE GOOD OF ALL.

7. GIVE CONSTANT THANKS TO THE GREAT SPIRIT EACH DAY

8. SPEAK THE TRUTH, BUT ONLY FOR THE GOOD OF OTHERS.

9. FOLLOW THE RHYTHMS OF NATURE

10. ENJOY LIFE'S JOURNEY BUT LEAVE NO TRACKS.

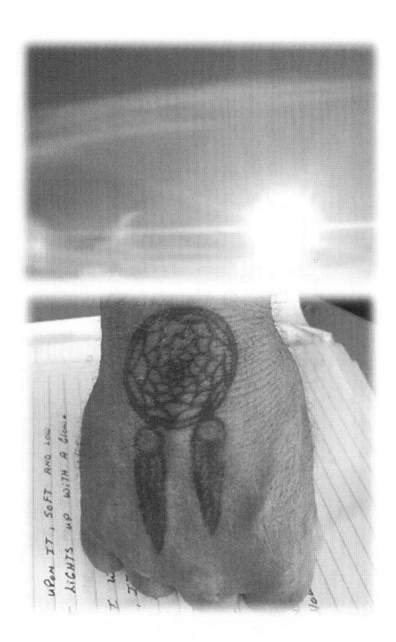

41

Made in the USA
Las Vegas, NV
09 July 2021